HOME OWNERSHIP:
A SUITABLE CASE FOR REFORM

Jack Woodward

Front cover photograph Rob Cowan
Designed by Janey Sugden/Artworkers
Printed by David Green Ltd, Kettering
Published in May 1986 by Shelter, 157 Waterloo Road, London SE1 8XF
Trade distribution by Turnaround 01 609 7836
ISBN 0 901242 71 3

HOME OWNERSHIP: A SUITABLE CASE FOR REFORM

MICHAEL BALL

Contents

Introduction

Owner-occupation is regarded by many as one of the success stories of post-war British housing policy. Over 60 per cent of households are now owner-occupiers, and the major political parties vie with each other in claiming that their policies can push up the percentage even further.

Yet, once all the rhetoric about property-owning democracy and the voting propensities of homeowners is pushed to one side, it has become clear to many observers that the current form of owner-occupied housing provision is beset with severe problems. Reform of the tenure is an urgent, if politically difficult, necessity.

What sort of reforms are required? The answer to that question depends on what are regarded as the key problems of owner-occupation. This book argues that the operations of housebuilders, building societies, and other institutions associated with owner-occupation must be a central focus of reform, and proposes a 10-point programme of reform summarized here:

1 Housebuilding by publicly accountable, non-profit bodies.

2 These new housebuilding enterprises to build for local housing needs while meeting agreed standards of quality and efficiency.

3 New forms of employment based on decasualization of building work, improved pay and conditions, and an emphasis on quality as much as speed of work.

4 Public ownership of land, with a new form of leasehold under which buildings may be owned.

5 Planned local programmes of new housebuilding, repair, improvement and redevelopment based on assessments of local housing need and the available resources.

6 New non-profit housing credit institutions dispensing funds to owner-occupiers and other housing institutions.

7 The new housebuilding and finance institutions to be publicly accountable and democratically controlled.

8 Reform of the exchange process, including the replacement of conveyancing by 'log book' leaseholds issued and updated by local housing exchange authorities which would co-ordinate all house sales and moves in other tenures.

9 Prices for new and second-hand housing to be set by the local housing exchange authority.

10 Mortgage tax relief to be limited to the first house purchase, together with the introduction of a 'sales tax' varied according to the rate of house price increase so as to discourage price rises and syphon off part of any inflationary gains made.

The experience of home ownership

One difficulty when talking about the problems of owner-occupation is that experiences of the tenure differ. Non-owners, for instance, may see owner-occupation as attractive, or as an excuse used by governments to avoid tackling their housing needs and a basis on which they are regarded as second-class citizens. Within owner-occupation, the experiences of households vary considerably. Some owners, though not as many as is often believed, have made substantial financial gains out of house price inflation and mortgage interest tax relief. Others face severe economic hardship as a result of purchase, and there is evidence to suggest that the proportion is growing.

Economic hardship arises for a variety of reasons. The initial years of purchase for many households are a severe strain. Alternatively, a large repair bill might threaten normal household finances.

But what is becoming increasingly clear is that systematic patterns of hardship exist among particular types of owner-occupier. As owner-occupation has become the only effective option for most British households, thousands have been drawn into and remain in a tenure which they can barely afford. In addition, many elderly owners find it difficult to finance the large irregular payments associated with outgoings like repair and maintenance. Marital breakdowns may cause mortgage foreclosures and severe financial hardship. The unemployed and long-term sick face the daunting task of trying to hang onto their homes, amongst their other worries. The numbers in each of these categories has been swelled by the general economic decline of recent years, especially in the worst hit regions of the country.

Each of these groups could be regarded as having isolated difficulties. The problems are essentially theirs and no-one else's. There are several reasons why this is untrue.

In the first place, transactions in the housing market are highly dependent on each other. If certain types of household get into difficulty, forced sales may start to push down the prices of all houses, as owner-occupiers in West Germany painfully discovered recently.

Not only do feedback effects reverberate throughout the housing market, implications also arise for the state of the overall housing stock. Recent house condition surveys have shown alarming increases in the extent of disrepair in owner-occupied dwellings. (The government is so concerned that it has changed the survey definitions, which means in future the problem will not look so bad.) Houses are falling into disrepair because their owners cannot afford to repair them, but in the end everyone will pay the cost of a dilapidated housing stock.

Finally, and most importantly, there are two sides to the problem of financially squeezed owner-occupiers. They cannot afford the costs of owner-occupation because these costs are so high, rather than just because their incomes are low. The costs of owner-occupation have risen considerably in recent years, because of rising interest rates and house prices. Meanwhile, the burden on the Exchequer of mortgage interest tax relief continues to grow uncontrollably.

A complex web ties all owner-occupiers to the vicissitudes of the housing market and to the institutions operating there. The following chapters will try to unravel that web. They will show that the current form of owner-occupied housing provision is in severe structural crisis. The problems of owners in financial difficulties is only one aspect of an increasingly rickety structure.

The contemporary structure of owner-occupied housing provision

Owner-occupied housing, as the name implies, simply means that the household owns the dwelling in which it lives. Such personal ownership, however, has become synonymous in Britain with housing provision via the private market. Instead, therefore, of simply being one way in which housing may be *consumed*, owner-occupation has become associated with a particular way in which housing is *provided*; and with all the forms of land-ownership, building, finance and market exchange that exist there. Together they constitute the contemporary structure of owner-occupied provision in Britain.

It is only possible to talk about specific historical forms of owner-occupation, rather than some abstract generality called 'owner-occupation'. No other Western European country, for example, has precisely the same form of owner-occupied housing provision as Britain.

In France and West Germany, for example, second-hand housing markets are fragmented and rarely linked to the new housing market: households generally do not move once they have bought a house. In Britain, on the other hand, second-hand sales and new sales are closely integrated in one general market. Trading-up is important in Britain, in France and Germany it is virtually non-existent.

The volume housebuilders dominate new housebuilding in Britain. In France, such builders were virtually wiped out in the mid-1970s; now most owner-occupied houses are built on single, occupier-owned plots. Many are prefabricated houses ordered from a catalogue. 'Self-building' is important in West Germany, and social housing institutions are major builders for owner-occupation.

In the Netherlands, mortgage banks are closely integrated with housing developers, and for years every new owner-occupied project had to be associated with the construction of some new social housing at the same location. In Sweden, state control of mortgage credit and land transactions puts an effective constraint on the level of house prices and housebuilding profits.

The variety of potential forms of owner-occupation can be extended way beyond those currently existing in Europe. There is no reason, for instance, why owner-occupation should be associated with a private, unregulated market. The final chapter will argue that owner-occupation in Britain would operate much better out of the straightjacket of the private market.

Once the structure of owner-occupied housing provision in Britain has been specified, it can be seen that the housing market operates like a transmission belt redirecting the costs and benefits of home-ownership. The housing market, for example, diffuses the effect of housing subsidies among a wide variety of beneficiaries. Mortgage tax relief enables the lenders of mortgages to charge higher interest rates than would otherwise be feasible. Similarly, the subsidy is partially transmitted through higher house prices to housebuilders' profits, landowners' revenues and the wealth of sellers of second-hand houses.

FIGURE 1. The structure of owner-occupied housing provision

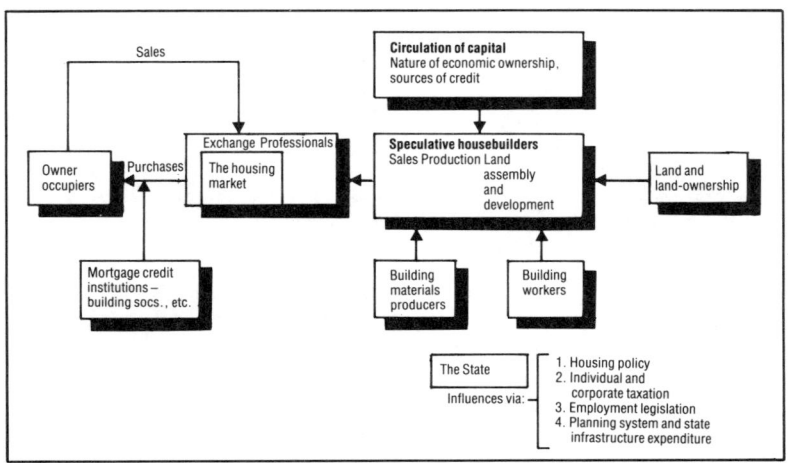

5

What the following chapters will do is to illustrate the extent to which the current nature of owner-occupation in Britain is a consequence of the social agents that dominate its structure of provision. It is easy to specify the agencies involved in owner-occupied housing provision, as is done in figure 1. But the linkages between them are not so clear cut, while changes in one part of the structure of provision generate complicated feedback in other parts. Understanding these feedback effects is the key to recognizing which aspects of the current structure of owner-occupation are most in need of reform, and so to providing certain guiding principles by which to formulate alternatives.

Substantial structural change is currently taking place within owner-occupied housing provision, particularly in the housing market itself and in housebuilding and mortgage finance. The following chapters will look at these processes of change in order to see how they are linked together, and how the structure of provision works.

Chapter 1

The workings of the owner-occupied housing market

An integrated market

The British owner-occupied housing market is a unified one. No distinct market for new houses exists, as is the case in many other Western European countries. Geographically, a spurt of house price inflation in one region is quickly reflected across the whole country. Over the past 20 years inter-regional population moves have been too great for the housing market in one region to be isolated from occurrences elsewhere.

Clear differences exist between the regions. Southern England has much higher house prices than elsewhere while the economically most dynamic localities have the most rapid housebuilding rates. But to date there is little evidence that such differences have lead to the creation of geographically distinct markets. The size of the United States means that California and the East Coast have separate housing markets. But Britain is too small and homogenous a country for such Balkanization to occur here. The widespread practices of trading-up and trading-down mean that even the most expensive types of housing are linked to the poorest through the mechanisms of the housing market.

The implications of such extensive integration are profound. Problems in one area quickly get transmitted through price and demand effects to other localities and house types, even if the consequences in different parts of the market vary. So problem sectors of the owner-occupied housing market are difficult to isolate. Run-down inner city owner-occupied housing, for instance, cannot be made independent of the market as a whole.

In this chapter, the workings of the owner-occupied market will be explored. The process of price determination will be looked at and an investigation made of why this housing market is so unstable. It will also be suggested that generally too much emphasis is put on demand considerations at the expense of the longer-run impact of supply. The detailed role of building societies is left to chapter 3. But here their influence on house prices is shown to be secondary rather than central, as is often claimed. Finally, something will have to be said about land prices – as it is frequently suggested that they determine the price of new housing.

House price changes

Much research energy has been expended trying to find out the determinants of house price rises. After considerable statistical analysis a broad consensus is emerging, although there is dis-agreement on the relative importance of some of the factors influencing price change. House price studies have found that in the short-term, the changes in the demand for owner-occupied housing overwhelmingly influence the rate of price change. Supply has only a longer-term effect. The principal influence on the short-term level of demand is the rate of change of real incomes (measured in various ways depending on the study in question). When incomes are rising, people can afford to spend more on housing and are able to undertake the tribulations and cost of moving home. As changes in real incomes are closely linked to the state of the economy as a whole, demand in the housing market is linked to the general level of economic activity.

A qualification must be made because of the way in which successive economic crises since the early 1970s have affected different types of household. Much of the burden of economic crisis has been pushed onto the unemployed (and the low waged). The UK owner-occupied housing market therefore has, to an extent, been shielded from the effects of the crisis and restructuring of the British economy. Owner-occupiers tend to be the economically-stronger households. New and existing owner-occupier house-holds' incomes have tended to fare better than the national average. In countries like West Germany, where most people's incomes have been strongly squeezed at times of economic crisis, the housing market (and house prices) have plummeted during recent recessions.

Other influences on demand, apart from income, are associated with the relative cost of house purchase. The rate of change of house prices is important, although its effect can be both negative and positive. As prices rise, less people are able to afford house purchase so demand is choked off. On the other hand, rising prices encourage some households to move, either to avoid higher prices in the future or because the houses they have to sell are also worth more.

The relative cost of living in other tenures and current mortgage interest rates also influence house prices. In both cases, however, their short-term effect appears to be weak. The cost of living in the principal alternative to owner-occupation, council housing, is determined mainly by long-term government strategies rather than short-term variations. The impact of changes in mortgage rates is weakened by the large number of variations in the mortgage rate over the past decade. By the time someone has gone through the whole transaction process of house purchase, the rate can easily have changed.

Mortgage credit availability is the final important short-term demand influence. Some commentators have adopted what could be described as a 'pure monetarist' stance, suggesting that the availability of mortgages is the sole influence on the rate of house price change. Such a position is not very sound. It implies that every house purchaser is credit rationed, yet the available evidence suggests that, apart from exceptional circumstances, relatively few are. In addition, the real costs of house ownership are ignored. Once a mortgage has been obtained it has to be paid off, so maximizing mortgage credit would for most households involve sharp reductions in their living standards. At best, it seems that credit availability has a significant effect only in specific time periods rather than a permanent influence.

Although the prime influences on demand and the rate of house price change are comparatively easy to discover, the exact influences are not. The effect of each influence is also likely to change over time, and with the stages in the cycle of activity in the market. Such variations and uncertainties create a field day for pundits, as they make accurate forecasting impossible.

An unstable market

The housing market is punctuated by booms, slumps and inter-
vening periods of stagnation. They show up clearly in the rate of
change of house prices, and in dramatic variations in the number
of house sales.

● House prices

At the end of the 1960s, after years of steady increase, house
prices began suddenly to fluctuate wildly, and they have not
stabilized again since then. As data on annual house price
changes from 1957–83 show (given in figure 2), real house prices
have varied the most, falling substantially in a number of years.

It is worth emphasizing that, after taking account of general
price inflation, house prices do not always rise. For example, the
1973 peak in real house prices, when house prices rose way
above the levels determined by usual economic influences, has
never been regained (see figure 3). Years of falling real house
prices combined with rising building costs help to explain why

FIGURE 2
House price changes per cent per annum 1957-85[1]

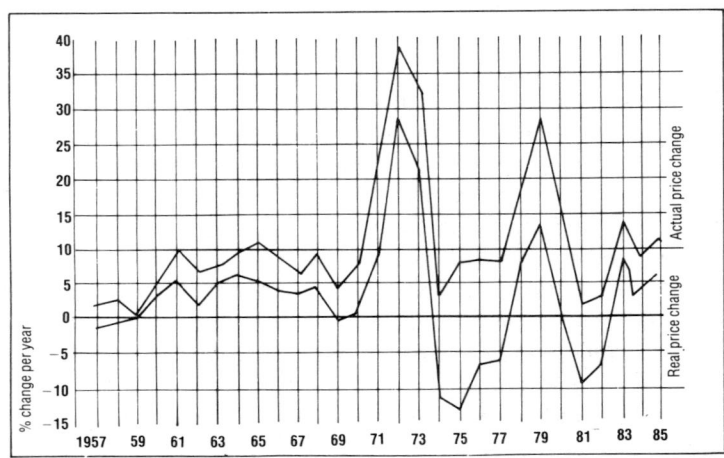

Source: Housing and Construction Statistics
[1] Prices at mortgage approval stage. See *BSA Bulletin* 19, p.21, for details of construction of house price
index

private housing output has tumbled in the 1980s to, on average, only half the 1960s' level.

Three major price booms have occurred since 1969: in 1972–73, 1978–79, 1984 and after. There is no evidence that price oscillations are levelling out in a return to the pattern of the 1960s. Although the peak of each price boom has been less than the previous one, this is principally a result of reduced general rates of inflation and a slower growth of real incomes during each successive economic upturn.

The latest housing boom has confounded the pundits who had argued that house price inflation was primarily caused by consumers treating owner-occupation as an attractive outlet for their investment funds. By the 1980s, negative real mortgage interest rates had disappeared and other potential investment outlets had become more attractive, yet still a house price boom took place.

In the 1960s, the housing market mainly served first-time buyers. Since then the role of existing owners has increased, and this transformation is the true cause of the market's inherent instability.

FIGURE 3
Index of annual real house prices 1969-1985

1969	1970	1971	1972	1973	1974	1975	1976	1977
76	77	80	98	121	115	100	92	85

1978	1979	1980	1981	1982	1983	1984	1985[1]
90	102	101	94	87	92	95	100

House Price Index deflated by Retail Price Index (1975 = 100).

1. Up to November.

Source: Economic Trends, Housing and Construction Statistics

FIGURE 4
Building society advances to existing and new owner-occupiers (quarterly)

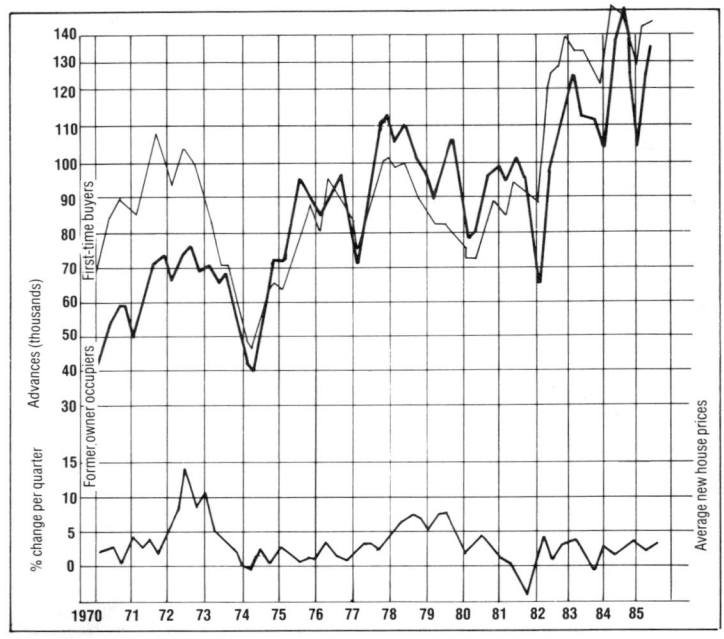

Source: BSA Bulletin

● Housing market transactions

In the space of six months or less, the number of transactions in the housing market can double or halve. Such dramatic changes show most starkly the instability of the housing market.

Indications of the changing pattern of moves by existing and new owners can be obtained by looking at the advances made each quarter by building societies. The advances are given quarterly from 1970-84 in figure 4. A steady growth in the number of loans to existing owners can be seen across the whole period, reflecting the increase in owner-occupation and the propensity of many owners in Britain to move frequently. Britain has one of the highest rates of mobility of existing owner-occupiers in the world. Home-owners move notably more frequently than in the USA, and far more frequently than in most other Western European countries. Home-owners' moves are not evenly spread over time. They bunch together during upturns in the market, reinforcing the cycle of boom and slump. Five such cycles have occurred since 1970—from 1970-74, 1974–76, 1977–79, 1980–81 and 1982 onwards.

Building societies do not fund all transactions. A small number of people buy outright and others borrow from banks and insurance companies, especially existing owners taking out larger mortgages. The lending activities of other financial institutions affect the accuracy of building society data in representing the true level of housing market activity, so the data in figure 4 do not always give a complete picture of market transactions. The renewed entry of the clearing banks into mortgage finance in 1981–82 removed a significant slice of the mortgage market from the building societies - depressing the existing owners' data for the 1980s. The remarkable spurt after 1981 in advances to first-time buyers shown in figure 4 reflects the building societies' enthusiasm for the Government's council house sales policy, rather than an increase in first-time buyers in the market.

Transactions can be looked at in terms of the types of dwellings purchased as well as the nature of the purchasers. This is done in figure 5. The long-term trend is one of falling purchases of new dwellings and rapidly increasing purchases of existing ones. Again, there are cyclical fluctuations and they are particularly marked for existing dwellings. Although housebuilders are capable of varying their output substantially, the scale of their operations is dwarfed by the total number of market transactions. (New housing took 25 per cent of the market in 1970 and only 12 per cent in 1983). Not surprisingly, therefore, fluctuations are greatest for existing dwellings.

It is worth considering why sales of existing dwellings fluctuate so much. Stock transfers from other tenures (which, apart from sales to council tenants, now run at around 50-60,000 a year) might be sensitive to variations in the state of the housing market. But it is to be expected that stock transfers are primarily influenced by longer-term considerations, like the need to gain

FIGURE 5
Building society advances on existing and new dwellings
1970-85 (quarterly)

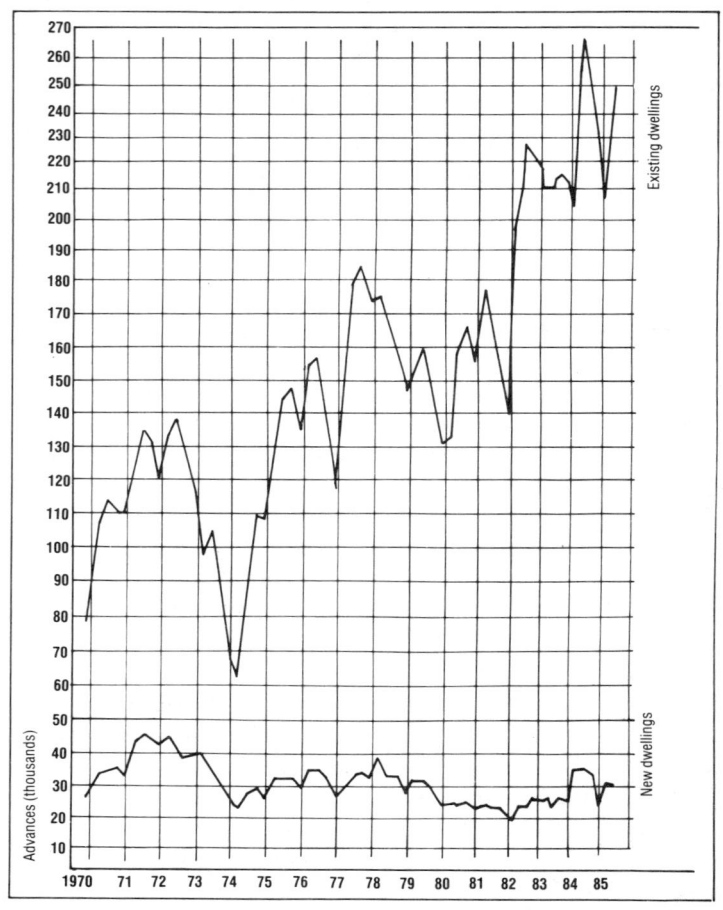

Source: BSA Bulletin

vacant possession of a rented dwelling before it can be sold into owner-occupation. Similarly, for about a third (on average) of the existing owner-occupied houses put on the market, sales arise from household dissolutions (through death, divorce and distress). But, again, the economics of the housing market only partially affect their numbers. The big short-term variations in the numbers of house sales transacted in the market arise because of existing owners who move.

If council house sales are excluded, roughly half of all the people buying owner-occupied houses are existing owner-occupiers. Surveys show that only about 15 per cent of them move because of changes in job location: most move to improve their housing situation – either locationally or in terms of housing standards. For existing owners, in particular, moves are dependent on attractive short-term economic conditions, so their moves tend to bunch together during upturns in the market. The reason is obvious: they can only move when they sell, and upturns in the market are the best time to sell.

As owner-occupation has expanded, the level of market transactions has become increasingly determined by the number of existing owners moving and, as a result, has become highly *unstable*. Upturns are heightened by an increase in existing owners wishing to move (particularly in order to trade-up), while downturns are strongly depressed by the withdrawal from the market of such movers.

Market instability is increased by the chains of sales in which existing owners who wish to move are involved. An existing owner has to sell a dwelling as well as purchase one. Where several existing owners are linked in the same chain of purchases and sales, the number of interlinked transactions can be substantial. A break in one part of the chain will halt all the purchases and sales associated with it. The extent of chains of sales should not be exaggerated. As about half the houses sold in a year are sold by existing owners wishing to move within owner-occupation, the average chain involves only two dwellings. Averages, of course, hide considerable variations – at one point in time and over time. So breaks in chains of sales can have a greater quantitative impact on total demand than the simple average implies. In particular, as more existing owners move during market upturns, chains are longer then and so more likely to break.

House price rises are not automatically associated with periods of increased transactions in the housing market. Prices get bidded up when demand outpaces additional supply. So, in order to understand the dynamic of the market, it is necessary to look at what has been happening to new housebuilding. The long-term trend of housing output has been falling for over 20 years. A lack of new housing output has helped to create the conditions in which excess demand, fuelled by the money gains of existing owners, can push up prices.

Building for the private housing market

Housebuilding firms are in business to make a profit. The cost of production, the timing of production and land assembly strategies all affect profitability as much as the state of demand and the prices at which houses can be sold. Through the ways in which they organise production and land assembly, builders can influence profitability. How each firm goes about doing this is considered in the next chapter. Here a few simple propositions about the aggregate level of output will be explored.

Private housebuilding has a relatively simple production process. Once a site has been acquired and serviced, it takes between two and six months to build a traditional house. This production period is sufficiently short for housebuilders to react quite quickly to changes in market conditions. Housebuilders, because of the costs of holding completed and semi-completed dwellings, have to be fairly sure when they start building a house that it will quickly sell at a profit. For this reason, production rates are geared closely to the level of sales. Selling prices are pitched at what the market will bear, with the proviso that production and land costs have to be covered.

In general, despite builders' protestations to the contrary, land purchase has little effect on the level of output during a market upturn. The time it takes to purchase land, obtain outline and detailed planning permission, and clear and service a site usually runs into years for all but the smallest sites. The reason is not much-complained about planning delays, but the sheer logistics of the land assembly operation itself. Negotiating with a landowner, passing through the legal process of land transfer and the physical preparation of a site are all activities that can take as long, if not longer, than the negotiation of planning permission.

Housebuilders in the short-term, therefore, have to dip into their stocks of building land (known as land banks) in order to build houses. For this reason, all but the smallest housebuilders hold a minimum of two to three years development land. The purchase price of that land will not reflect current land costs as it was purchased in earlier years. Contemporary land purchases by builders generally reflect future rather than current output intentions.

Short-term variations in profitability result primarily from differences in the rate of change of house prices and building costs. When building costs race ahead of house prices, profitability falls, and vice versa. The difference can be defined as the *rate of change of development profitability*. Comparing the change in development profitability with variations in the aggregate number of dwellings produced on a quarterly basis since the early 1970s suggests that the two are closely correlated. When profitability rises, output rises; when profitability falls, output falls. No more sophisticated theory – like one that tries to assess housebuilders' expectations – is required to explain housing output because of the way production is organized, the relatively short time it takes to build a house, and the high cost of stock holding.

FIGURE 6
Quarterly changes in new house prices and construction costs, 1970-85

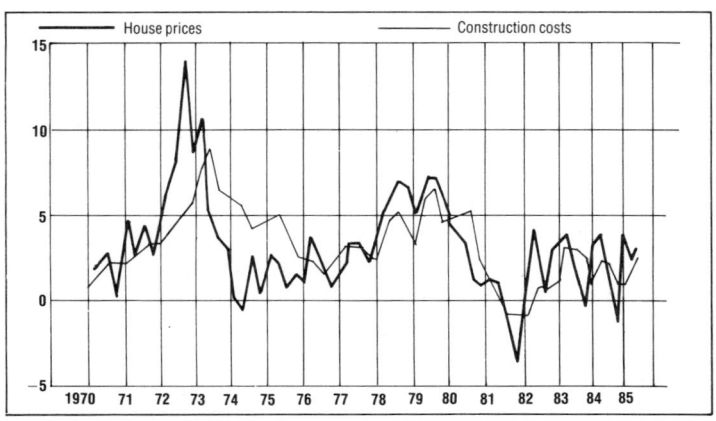

Sources: New house price and private new housing output price indices, HCS

During the 1970s, as figure 6 shows, only at the peaks of the house price booms of 1972–73 and 1979–80 did house prices rise significantly faster than construction costs. Even in those booms, new output was choked off by rising construction costs. The long-term rise in construction costs helps to explain why private housing output has declined so dramatically since the 1960s. It simply is not profitable to build any more houses. House prices would over the long term have had to rise even faster than they have in order to induce more output.

Land prices

Land prices are frequently said to push up house prices and limit the supply of new housing. While in particular localities that argument may be true, there is no evidence that it holds for the market as a whole. Residential land prices are determined by demand. Housebuilders are the ones buying the land and, not surprisingly, the price they are prepared to pay depends on the profitability of building on that land. This simple economic relationship between land prices and the profitability of land use has been known since at least the time of Adam Smith. All the available data suggest that the price of residential building land, with a few lags, responds closely to the profitability of housebuilding. Similarly, there is no evidence that aggregate housing output has been influenced by land shortages – the profitability of housebuilding instead seems to be the principal factor determining output.

Landowners know they are onto a good thing with private housebuilding and are incapable of colluding against the large housebuilders to hold large amounts of land off the market. Landowners just sit back and enjoy their enormous unearned increments. It would be interesting to know how many million-aires have been made out of people owning land near the new M25. Unfortunately, there is no way of finding out. For genera-tions, land ownership data have been suppressed to stop public outcries over the enormous financial gains from land ownership. Landowners do not want to bankrupt builders. Cosy arrange-ments with them are far more profitable. And planners make a wonderful scapegoat for both landowner and builder.

Chapter 2

The volume housebuilders: coping with crisis

Dramatic changes have occurred in speculative housebuilding over the past 20 years. A handful of giant firms have come to dominate what was previously a fragmented industry. These firms have totally different strategies towards marketing, land assembly and production than the old-style local firms. The consequences have been substantial for the numbers of new owner-occupied houses built, their quality, who they are built for, and their cost.

The volume housebuilders have won against their smaller competitors because they are more capable of dealing with the modern housing market. Yet prospects for many of them look bleak over the next few years. The housing market is likely to move into one of its cyclical downturns, and the industry has been wracked by criticisms of high-pressure selling techniques, poor quality, and the new timber-frame building method. The volume builders can hardly be said to have cracked the problem of providing good quality, low cost housing. As we shall see, the reverse has happened – they have helped exacerbate a crisis of housing production.

What do speculative housebuilders do?

Speculative housebuilders build housing for the general market rather than for a known client. In Britain, they control the whole process of land development, design, building and sales.

Builders have a series of interrelated speculative calculations to make. They include:

- when and where to buy land, and should it be bought with or without planning permission?
- what sector of the housing market to aim for?
- what external design or internal features should the houses have?
- when to build (which requires guesses about future trends in the housing market and in building costs)?
- and, finally, at what price should the dwelling be sold?

Each of these decisions involves considerable risk.

Housebuilders adopt particular strategies to reduce risk. Some of the strategies lead to the choosing of specific organizational structures and operating rules in the spheres of land assembly, site development and housing production. Detailed local knowledge of housing and land markets and of local building gangs is required for success. Each volume builder consequently operates on the basis of local regional subsidiaries. These regional subsidiaries have a small headquarters staff and are organised to produce an optimal output of somewhere between 250 and 1,000 homes. If output expands so do the number of subsidiaries; if it falls they contract. Barratt's housebuilding subsidiaries, for example, fell from 33 to 25 in 1984 because of its well-publicized troubles. As special managerial skills are required in speculative housebuilding, few of the subsidiaries take on other building work. Generally, they are purely spec builders.

No other country has a housebuilding industry quite like Britain's. In many other countries, a large part of the market is taken up by individual owners buying a plot of land and then hiring building workers or a building company to build a house for them. Virtually all French owner-occupied housing is of this individualized form, and much of Australia's, West Germany's and the USA's. In Britain, in contrast, almost all new houses are bought from speculative builders. They dominate housing production. No-one else can match the land prices they can pay, while planners frown on single plot sales because of the scattered forms of development they create.

Planners have not deliberately aided the large builders, but have encouraged block land release to meet the (highly desirable) planning goals of compact suburban development to minimize environmental effects and to bring order to the large-scale expenditure by the state on infrastructure. Individual housebuilders and their national lobbies are unlikely to thank the planners because they are still forbidden, like everyone else, from building at particular locations. If speculative builders could build at some of the more choice locations banned by the planners, and nobody else could, they would make enormous profits. So housebuilders always have an incentive to bite the planning hand that helps to sustain them.

Who owns the volume builders?

Volume housebuilders (those building 500 or more houses) produced only about 15 per cent of new owner-occupied houses in 1969. By the mid-1980s they were producing over half the owner-occupied output. The thousands of petty capitalist builders who build 10 or less houses a year were hardly affected by the volume builders' growth. Their market share has stayed at around the 10–15 per cent level. Small and medium-sized capitalist builders, instead, have disappeared. Many of them have been acquired by bigger enterprises, and even among the largest firms takeovers have swallowed up many companies.

Housebuilders buy up other housebuilders to acquire their stocks of land. In this way, a builder can grow rapidly, particularly in a new region of operation. Also, much of the land acquired in this way will be exceedingly cheap. Barratt grew from being a tiny North-East firm in the late 1960s to Britain's largest housebuilder in the 1980s by pursuing an active takeover policy. Tarmac, the third largest housebuilder, did not build a single house until 1973, when it bought up a virtually bankrupt housebuilder and then poured capital into expanding it.

Looking at the ownership patterns, it can be seen that some housebuilders are part of large construction firms operating across different sectors of the construction industry (such as Wimpey and Tarmac) or by giant conglomerates which stretch their activities across a wide number of industries as well as construction (such as Trafalgar House and P & O). Other housebuilders are controlled by wealthy private families. Some have entered speculative housebuilding as an attractive investment outlet (for instance, the Salveson family, one of the richest in

Scotland). Others have become rich through the profits derived from building – Bellway, Wilson Connolly, and Beazer are all of this type. Barratt is an exception in that its founder now owns only a tiny proportion of the company, although speculative housebuilding has made Laurie Barratt a very wealthy man. Barratt Developments, instead, has been able to raise enormous sums of capital through periodic rights issues on the Stock Exchange – capitalizing on the company's buoyant share price prior to its recent troubles.

Who owns the volume builders has been an important element in their success. Volume builders have access to plentiful long-term development capital through their ownership structures. Their investment plans are not constrained by the profits they are currently making or the whim of a jittery bank manager. The volume builders have the resources to mount extensive marketing campaigns. They can spread their presence over large regions and operate in many different sectors of the housing market – starter and up-market, retirement and holiday, inner city and suburban, rehabilitation and new. In this way, the risks of failed schemes on overall profitability can be minimized and advantage taken of shifts in market trends. Output can be trimmed during tight market conditions rather than having to accept large reductions in profit margins on house sales. One or two years' bad profits can easily be outweighed by longer-term growth prospects. Losses can be borne on projects that heighten the firm's market image. Most importantly, they can buy land at times of depressed conditions, acquire large tracts that can be developed only over a number of years, and take over other builders.

The current ownership structure of the major producers has been one of the principal reasons why speculative house-building has been transformed over the past 20 years – away from its small-time builder image of the 1950s and 60s to a larger scale marketing and land-development orientated exercise. Notice that the new long-term sources of capital have been put to work on marketing, land-development and takeover. It has not been used extensively to buy new productive equipment (most of which is hired rather than owned) or invested in new building techniques. Even timber-frame building was introduced only because it saved on productive capital, and most timber-frame systems are sold to housebuilders rather than directly produced by them.

The attractiveness of investing in housebuilding has been enhanced by Britain's tax laws. The volume housebuilders have paid little tax for many years. In addition, public infrastructure investment and the granting of planning permission on land speculatively bought bring substantial tax-free land development gains. Development land tax, like previous attempts at taxing land gains, proved worthless in practice. Though much fuss has been made over mortgage interest tax relief, the proportionately much greater tax reliefs on housebuilders' profits have excited no comment. The current reforms of corporation tax will reduce some of the present tax benefits, but many will still remain. Yet is is unlikely that the lax tax regime of housebuilders has led to any more houses being built, as the reliefs are primarily associated with land dealing rather than production. Tax considerations, by encouraging firms to buy and hold more land, are likely to have pushed up land prices as well.

Risky business

The volume housebuilders have managed to reduce the risks of producing for a volatile housing market. They even profit from the housing market's ups and downs. But success depends on making correct guesses of future trends in both the housing and land markets, locally as well as nationally. The managements of volume housebuilders are skilled in acquiring market information and juggling with the various calculations required to get a maximum return. But, ultimately, they have to hope that their guesses are right. The speculative nature of housebuilding extends from the purchase of a site, through the timing of its development to the overall output and investment strategies of the firm as a whole. In recent years, some firms – such as Bryant and Tarmac – have done remarkably well. Others have fared badly; Barratt and Wimpey, the two largest housebuilders, are among them.

Wimpey's troubles started in the late 1970s, when senior management failed to spot the new trends in marketing, land development and the organization of production. Wimpey's output tumbled by almost a third in three years from a peak of

11,000 homes in 1979, while arch rival, Barratt, continued to forge ahead.

Barratt's problems arrived much later in 1983. After years of growth, Barratt's output started to fall and profits tumbled. The company has blamed the barrage of criticism it has received in the media over hard-selling techniques – especially related to first-time buyers purchasing rapidly depreciating domestic equipment – and fears about the structural viability of its timber-framed houses. The company must have been surprised at being singled out for these criticisms, as most volume builders have done the same. Laing, for instance, built 100 per cent timber-frame houses and its sales surged ahead at the same time as Barratt's were slumping. A recent *Which* report, in July 1984, suggested that house purchasers think most volume builders are as bad as each other – 75 per cent of those surveyed had problems with their new houses. Barratt is paying the price of the high media profile it had so carefully nurtured earlier, aimed at making people associate private housebuilding with Barratt. Yet is unlikely that Barratt's problems stem solely from poor publicity. Much of its difficulties are likely to arise from over-ambitious expansion plans and a mistaken belief that the company could always buck downturns in the housing market. It is difficult for the largest producer in a market not to be affected by a general slackening of demand. The years of expansion through the cheap acquisition of strickened builders and through advances over competitors in marketing techniques have come to an end. Output now can only be increased significantly through internal growth, in a context where competitors' sales techniques have caught up. The problems of Barratt look set to remain for a number of years to come.

One final example of a volume housebuilder, Comben Homes, illustrates the role of long-term development capital and the penalties of misjudging the market – twice. Comben has a history stretching back to before the First World War. It came badly unstuck with the collapse of the early 1970s housing boom. Hawker Siddley acquired the company in 1978, using part of the compensation from the state for the nationalization of its aircraft manufacturing business. Almost immediately after its takeover, Comben went on a buying spree, acquiring a number of other housebuilders and gaining a significant presence in most regions, apart from the South-East. Hawker's investment in housebuilding looked like it would soon pay off. But Comben failed to diversify throughout all sectors of the housing market – remaining an up-market producer alone. The slump of the early 1980s hit the company badly: it failed to move down market sufficiently quickly and was not represented in the still buoyant South-East region. In early 1984, the company seemed to have realized its mistakes and announced plans to have a much greater first-time buyer presence. But by that time Hawker Siddley had become disenchanted with its speculative house-building venture and sold Comben to Trafalgar House in the summer of 1984.

A structural crisis of production

In recent years there have been significant changes in the organization of housing production. While some of them constitute major transformations of on-site production, the current relationship of volume builders to their casualized workforce has led to what can only be called a structural crisis of housing production.

Small-batch production of dissimilar house types has become the norm on most private housing sites. Building workers operate almost entirely as casualized, self-employed operatives, either individually or in gangs (a practice commonly known as the Lump). Most plant and equipment is hired or brought onto site by a subcontractor.

Even with traditional brick and block building methods, many previous site tasks have been reduced to simple assembly operations. Most woodworking is now done in factories. Items such as prefabricated staircases and roof trusses have over the past 15 years or so replaced complex on-site woodworking tasks. Fork-lift trucks and mechanical diggers have virtually obliterated the previously heavy manual work of lifting and digging. Ready-mixed concrete can be ordered and pumped where required, and houses are designed in ways which simplify building tasks as much as possible.

Private housebuilding cannot be regarded as technically moribund. Firms are aware of the extra profits to be made from reducing production costs, and where possible react accordingly. Modern production management philosophies, aided by the ubiquitous computer, can be applied to the flow of workers, machines and materials on a private housing site.

For the individual firm, however, minimizing production costs has to be subordinated to other profit-maximizing requirements. Volume builders need their output to be spread across a large number of sites to take advantage of different market segments. And the fickleness of demand in any geographic or house-type market sector discourages firms from building much ahead of the rate of sales on any particular site. Working capital tied up in uncompleted houses or site infrastructure can be disastrous if demand collapses. Hence, small-batch production is the rule. Hiring self-employed workers on a piece-rate basis similarly lowers overhead costs. Piece rates have the added advantage of fixing the pace at which workers undertake their tasks, minimizing the need for supervision.

Limitation of working capital puts enormous pressure on the speed at which building work is done. Lump workers want to work quickly to maximize their earnings, while firms want houses completed fast so that they can be sold. The quality of work suffers on both counts. An additional problem is that the rapid production of a few houses on each site limits the economies of scale that can be achieved. The advantage of rationalized production therefore get dissipated in poor quality and small-scale.

What is rational for the individual firm in the short-run, moreover, can have some perverse effects on production as a whole, which then rebound back on each enterprize. Subcontracting is a clear case of this paradox. Individual firms subcontract building work on a supply-and-fix or labour-only basis because subcontracting reduces production costs. But subcontracting helps to weaken building firms' control over the terms and conditions under which building workers and plant can be hired. Subcontractors are notorious for not turning up at the agreed time. It frequently is not in their interests to do so, for, as punctual subcontractors, they are likely to face more idle time between jobs than those who bend timings to their own benefit. When the demand for building work is strong, this disruptive effect is likely to be greatest. Similarly, subcontracting may reduce the overall supply of building workers and plant because all firms avoid their obligations to train labour and to make sure building equipment exists. The end result is that, over the long-term, the growth of speculative building – and especially the volume housebuilders – has exacerbated a skills crisis in the building industry. Skilled labour shortages appear in particular localities, even though there is mass unemployment of construction workers nationally, while the collapse of training leads to a gradual decline in standards of work.

An outcome of the changes in the organization of production over the past decade or so is that building firms cannot meet sudden increases in housing demand. The production process becomes more disjointed at times of boom as subcontractors overcommit themselves and housebuilding firms, frantic for output to sell, competitively bid-up subcontract rates. Rising costs begin to choke off the extra profits created by house price increases, and output starts to fall away. In slumps, the reverse occurs – production becomes easier and cheaper. But then, no-one wants to buy houses, and volume builders stampede after first-time buyers in an attempt to drum up sales.

Real building costs are rising over the long-term, with cyclical variations of rising costs in upturns and falling costs in down-turns. This suggests that the negative effects of the volume builders' concern to reduce the costs of production far outweigh the positive ones.

Chapter 3

The building societies step out

The past few years have been remarkably good ones for the building societies. A threat from the clearing banks in the mortgage market has been headed off, at least temporarily. A harmonious debate amongst the societies over future diversification strategies has been undertaken. A government Green Paper, published in 1984, promised virtually all the legislative changes the societies wanted. To cap it all, the mortgage market – after years in the doldrums – took off in 1982, and building societies were able to attract sufficient new funds to issue a record number of new mortgages. Between 1981 and the middle of 1984, the real value of the societies' mortgage business rose by almost 30 per cent – a rate of growth not experienced since the boom years of 1971–73. Once again, for the building societies, owner-occupation has become a major engine of growth: a firm base from which to launch their ambitious plans to become general financial services and property market institutions.

Unfortunately, unlike the old adage about General Motors and the USA, what has been good for the building societies has not necessarily been good for anyone else. Investors with the societies have received a fillip from the heady interest rate competition among the societies. And the government has been saved the acute embarrassment of having to fund its own council house sales programme. But owner-occupiers have had to face higher mortgage interest charges because of the record rates offered to savers and the loans granted to council tenants. As many investors with building societies are also owner-occupiers, even the higher savings rates offered to investors have for many been partly offset by higher mortgage costs.

Meanwhile, the societies' high interest rate policies have bumped up the cost of mortgage interest tax relief to the Exchequer and the taxpayer. Last, but by no means least, there has been a marked increase in the level of mortgage debt in the housing market. The increase in the ratio of mortgage debt to house prices is especially noticeable for existing owners. In the future, it may spell disaster for many owner-occupiers and building societies.

This chapter looks at why the building societies and the mortgage market are changing so fast. It suggests that owner-occupiers are not benefitting from the changes.

Why have building societies grown so fast?

Building societies are friendly societies acting as financial intermediaries between savers and mortgagees. As friendly societies, technically they are non-profit-making and have limits on what they can do, as laid down in a succession of Building Society Acts. Overseeing the movement is the Chief Registrar of Friendly Societies, who has the power to close down societies contravening the rules (as occurred with the New Cross Building Society in January 1984).

Building societies do not have to be of a particular size, in terms of the assets they hold, nor do they need to grow. Evidence on building society costs per £100 of assets shows that the largest five societies do seem to gain some economies of scale as they have the lowest per unit operating expenses. But, for the bulk of societies, growth does not improve efficiency in terms of lowering operating costs.

The largest societies are monster organizations with over £5,000 million assets each. Their size makes them remote from the building society ideal of a mutual society from which investors and borrowers directly benefit, and have a considerable say in the running of its affairs. The hundred or so largest societies operate like any capitalist financial institution, except that shareholders do not have to be appeased with dividend payments from large profits. Senior management in building societies can determine policy, virtually unconstrained by shareholders or by fear of a predatory takeover. Many mergers occur between building societies, but, unlike ordinary firms, they do not threaten the management of the absorbed society. A merger can only occur if both societies' managements want it. Persuasion, by the offer of good new jobs or attractive severance payments, is the main way of convincing a society's management that a merger is a good thing. The frantic scramble for growth by all the societies only makes sense in terms of its benefits to management. The advantages to anyone else are difficult to find.

While the rationale for expansion may lie with management, conditions must exist which enable expansion to occur. To an extent, building societies have been able to expand because of their privileged legal and tax position (such as low corporation tax, limited monetary policy constraints, and the composite taxation arrangements for investors' interest). Principally, however, building societies can expand because of their role in the owner-occupied market. They dominate owner-occupier mortgage lending, even if other financial institutions, like banks, have made occasional forays into their patch.

Building society dominance of mortgage lending from the 1930s onwards led to owner-occupied housing finance becoming a relatively 'closed' circuit. The societies borrow from the personal sector and lend to others in the personal sector, without the intervention of any other financial institution or market. The relative interest rates offered by building societies determine what proportion of personal sector liquid assets end up in that financial circuit rather than with banks or the Exchequer (the societies' principal competitors).

Getting in the money

Building societies have been able to grow because they have offered more attractive interest rates to investors than their competitors. In 1963, the societies attracted only 21 per cent of personal sector liquid assets; in 1984, their most successful year, the proportion had risen to over 50 per cent of a much larger sum. Those rates could be given to investors because of the strong demand by new and existing owner-occupiers for mortgages. Expansion of the movement as a whole, in other words, has depended on the buoyancy of the owner-occupied housing market. Recent periods of rapid growth for the societies have

FIGURE 7.
Building societies: societies, branches and assets

NUMBER OF SOCIETIES

1900	1930	1940	1950	1960	1970	1980	1985
2,286	1,026	952	819	726	481	273	167

NUMBER OF BRANCHES

1968	1970	1972	1974	1976	1978	1980	1982	1984
1,662	2,016	2,552	3,099	3,696	4,595	5,716	6,480	6,816

NUMBER OF BORROWERS (million)

1940	1950	1960	1970	1975	1981	1983	1984
1,503	1,508	2,349	3,655	4,397	5,484	5,928	6,314

TOTAL ASSETS (£m.)

1940	1960	1970	1975	1980	1983	1984
756	3,166	10,819	24,204	53,793	85,868	102,689

MORTGAGES OUTSTANDING (£m.)

	1960	1970	1973	1975	1977	1979	1981	1983	1984
Actual	2,647	8,752	14,532	18,802	26,427	36,801	48,854	67,490	81,882
Deflated to 1975 prices (deflator RPI)	7,272	16,207	21,122	18,802	19,590	22,900	22,400	27,148	31,384

% of building society assets held in 1981 by:

Top 2	Top 5	Top 10
35	55	71

Source: BSA Bulletin, Wilson Committee (1980), BSA (1981)

occurred when both transactions and prices in the housing market were booming. When the market is sluggish, real growth stops and even turns negative (figure 7).

Building societies are locked into the fortunes of the owner-occupied housing market because of its effect on the inflow of funds as well as its impact on the demand for mortgages. It has been calculated that on average about two-thirds of building societies' income is derived from the owner-occupied market. Mortgage interest and repayments of principal are two obvious sources. Repayments of principal rise substantially during market upturns when existing owners cash in their current mortgages and take out new, and usually larger, ones. New money paid into investors' accounts has often come from the sale of an owner-occupied dwelling. It is worthwhile seeing where it comes from.

Varying but substantial amounts of investors' deposits with building societies are larger sums of £2,000 plus. In 1977, for instance, 69 per cent of the societies' net receipts were such large sums, but only 33 per cent in 1979. These larger sums are generally thought to be 'new' money rather switches of funds from competitors. Such large investments can only come from realized personal sector wealth, half of which is represented by the net value of owner-occupied houses. A significant part of the receipts of last-time sellers (mainly 'dissolved households') and the money gains realized by existing owners consequently end up in investment accounts with building societies. No firm evidence is available to examine the relative importance of such realized wealth over time, but its volume is likely to be greatest during booms. The ability of building societies to lend mortgages, in other words, is closely related to the state of the housing market. Housing market booms help to generate the mortgage funds that sustain them, while slumps can lead to a contraction of credit.

The interest rate balancing act

For building societies to expand, their interest rates not only have to match those of other savings outlets but be more attractive. The societies have to undertake a careful balancing act of trying to set investors' interest rates above those of competitors, without making mortgages prohibitively expensive or enabling other financial institutions, like the clearing banks, to enter the mortgage market.

Building societies have been in the main very successful with their interest rate balancing act. The introduction of differential interest rates to investors and borrowers in the mid-1970s helped considerably to stabilize and increase the inflow of funds. Differential mortgage interest rates enable them to discriminate against certain types of borrower (especially those taking out larger mortgages) in order to finance the higher savings rates. Until 1983, the societies' interest rate cartel stopped interest rate competition from spilling over into the movement itself.

Higher interest rates, however, have a double-edged effect. Once having offered them to investors, building societies become locked into a relatively high interest rate regime, and they have to find people who are willing to borrow their more expensive funds. At the same time, mortgage borrowing from competing institutions, like the banks, is made more attractive. When the housing market is booming and the government is selling off lots of council houses, no problem exists as the demand for mortgage funds is high. When the market slumps, the dilemmas start to mount and the societies may end up with nowhere to lend their money. Such a prospect almost became reality in 1981–82, when the banks at one stage took 40 per cent of new mortgage business, forcing the building societies to abandon temporarily their mortgage interest rate differentials. This fear of insufficient outlets is a major reason for the societies' current attempts to diversify away from the housing market.

The interest rate dilemma has been exacerbated in recent years by the increase in competition between the societies as they compete for savings and jockey for a position in the restructuring of the bigger societies into general financial institutions. Competitive pressures between building societies over interest rates led in 1983 to the abandonment of the interest rate fixing cartel. Since then the societies have been involved in a competitive leap-frogging of interest rates offered to investors, with the result that mortgage rates have had to remain high. Even a recent chairperson of the Building Societies Association, Herbert Walden, recognized in a public speech that the main effect of such competition was to raise mortgage interest rates. As diversification gets underway, competition will intensify – putting further pressure on societies' operating costs. Every society will have to compete expensively for new forms of business, each one unable to go against the trend because of the fear of a rapid loss of business as customers switch to other more attractive societies.

The need for profits

One difficulty facing building societies as they expand is that they need to maintain a prudent ratio of reserves to total assets. Reserves can only be built up through retained profits, which are shown as surpluses in their annual accounts. Societies bent on rapid expansion need to make considerable profits to boost reserves sufficiently. In the past, dealing in the government securities market provided the societies which much of their profit. The favourable tax treatment of building societies in the gilt-edged market was abolished early in 1984. Pressure was then thrown on to the societies to find more profit out of their operating margins and to dabble in higher risk, higher return investments – exactly the area where the New Cross Building Society came unstuck.

Originally, in the Spalding Report of 1982, the societies wanted to be able to set up separate subsidiaries to deal in profitable but high risk areas. If things went wrong the subsidiaries could be closed down, with little effect on the parent society. The savings and loan associations in the USA have used subsidiaries to enter high risk investment areas and to hive off their worst-performing mortgages. Nobody knows quite what the building societies will do and at present it is unclear what the legal position regarding subsidiaries will be. Fears over the possible misuse of subsidiaries highlight the general point that the Government's current proposals for building society legislative reform contain few safeguards against investment gambles. The importance of profit for expansion could persuade a number of society managers to take unnecessary investment risks. It has happened elsewhere with deregulation. In the USA, the largest savings and loan institution, the FCA Corporation, almost went bankrupt early in 1984. Others in Ohio and Maryland folded in 1985, threatening the whole US financial system. Similarly, in West Germany a number of financial institutions associated with the housing market have made some extremely rash investments. The new role of the building societies could threaten the British financial system in a similar way.

The rising mortgage debt burden

Mortgage debt as a proportion of total house price has been rising significantly over the past few years. The rise is particularly noticeable for existing owners. In 1980, only 46 per cent of purchase price on average was funded by a mortgage, the rest came from savings and money realized from the sale of a previous house. By early 1984, the proportion borrowed had risen to 59 per cent of purchase price. The rise is all the more remarkable when compared to the pattern during the 1970s. During periods of rising housing prices in the early and late 1970s, existing owners were flush with the money gains realized from the sale of their previous dwellings and the proportion of purchase prices funded by a mortgage fell during house price booms, only to rise again in the next downturn. Yet, when house prices started to rise rapidly in 1983, the percentage advance rose rather than fell. To use the Bank of England's terminology, in the 1980s there has been a large-scale withdrawal of 'equity' from owner-occupation.

First-time buyers are also taking out bigger mortgages, although the rise is less dramatic as they have always borrowed a high proportion of purchase price. In 1979, their percentage advance had reached a long-term low of 74 per cent; in 1982–85, it reached a high of 85 per cent.

The rise in mortgage debt is open to a number of interpretations. It has been suggested that the increase results from the end of the era of mortgage shortages. Existing owners are no longer forced to re-invest all of their money gains, and have pushed up their borrowings to optimal amounts. This argument has serious weaknesses. It is difficult to believe that mortgages were permanently scarce for decades: consumer surveys in the 1970s, for instance, indicated that many people did not want a higher mortgage than they had obtained. In addition, mortgage queues reappeared temporarily in 1983–84 but existing owners' percentage advances did not fall in consequence. Rather than argue that owner-occupiers were previously severely constrained in their mortgage borrowing activities, it seems more plausible to say that the increase in mortgage debt helped to fuel the consumer boom of 1982–85. The advantage of diverting mortgage credit to general expenditure is considerable – as a comparison between the net-of-tax mortgage interest rate and that charged by a hire purchase or credit card company shows.

Increases in mortgage debt have had their effect on mortgage/income ratios. For existing owners, after years of decline, the average mortgage income ratio rose by 18 per cent between 1980 and 1984. For first-time buyers, it rose by 12 per cent. Although emphasis is generally put on the burden of mortgages to first-time buyers in the early years of purchase, in fact, the average mortgage/income ratio is similar for first-time buyers and existing owners when taking out a new mortgage, (1.86 and 1.81 respectively in the first quarter of 1985).

A qualification to the increase in the mortgage debt ratio should be made. The ratios have still not risen to their levels in the early 1970s housing boom. But in the early 1970s, with the high rates of inflation then existing, owner-occupiers could confidently assume that the real burden of their mortgage debt would fall rapidly. In the mid-1980s, with lower rates of inflation, the real burden of an equivalent mortgage/income ratio is much greater. Owner-occupiers now have less financial leeway than for many years – they face higher real debt burdens and have more of the value of their houses on mortgage. If the British economy goes into another major downturn, as it may do over the next few years, many owner-occupiers could be in trouble.

Building societies and council house sales

During the 1980s, over half a million council houses have been sold. Many sales were financed with building society mortgages. In 1982, 75,000 sales were financed in this way – giving the societies an extra £700m of business, nine per cent of the year's total advances. In 1983, advances to council tenants rose to £2,000m, over 10 per cent of total advances. A considerable proportion of building societies' recent record growth has consequently resulted from the Government's council house sales programme.

As the building societies are keen to tell everyone, they have not been able to reduce mortgage interest rates because of the high demand for mortgages – yet take the council house mortgage advances out of the sum and the demand is not so high. Without the council house sales programme, building societies would have had to restrict their inflow of funds by cutting interest rates, enabling an equivalent reduction in mortgage interest rates. *All owner-occupiers with mortgages have ended up paying higher mortgage interest rates because of council house sales.* Not only remaining council tenants but also owner-occupiers have had to pay the cost of the Government's anti-council housing stance.

Institutional change in the mortgage market

The clearing banks only caught on to the profitability of mortgage lending in the late 1970s, having traditionally emphasized corporate customers and overseas lending. Their German counterparts had noticed much earlier and acquired all of Germany's private mortgage banks in the early 1970s – a move which, at least initially, turned out to be very profitable.

After an initial flurry in 1982–83, when the banks took 40 per cent of the new mortgage market, the presence of the banks has been muted. They now lend about 25 per cent of all new mortgages, although the absolute drop in their mortgage advances is not as great because of the effect on the proportion of the general upturn in mortgage lending. The increased competition in the mortgage market has had little direct effect on building societies, because the recent boom in the housing market and the bonanza of council house sales have enabled the societies to keep their interest rates high. The effect of competition from the banks will only become apparent again during the next downturn in the housing market.

Building societies, in turn, also want to confront the clearing banks on their traditional territory. The societies have reached the limits of their ability to expand through lending out mortgages to owner-occupiers, so they want to diversify into general banking and real estate activities.

The moves of the banks into mortgage lending and the attempts of the building societies to diversify have forced the Government into action in the taxation and legislative fields. Since 1983, virtually all of the societies' special tax advantages over the clearing banks have been removed. Restrictions on building society activities are, at the same time, being weakened considerably: a Green Paper was published in 1984 (*Building societies: a new framework* Cmnd 9316), and legislation will be enacted in 1986 which gives the societies just about all they wished for.

Competition between the banks and the building societies is bound to intensify over the next few years which will encourage even further centralization amongst both institutions. Some societies may even abandon their friendly society status and merge with other financial institutions. Late in 1985, for instance, the Abbey National said it was contemplating a share issue once it became legally possible. Several banks have also made it known that they would like to own a building society.

Borrowers will not gain from competition. The societies desire to diversify, after all, in order to avoid adopting expansion strategies in owner-occupation alone, which would require them to reduce the powers of selectivity that they exercise so effectively now. To attract more business, they might even have had to offer better deals to minority groups and/or lower interest rates.

Chapter 4

Signs of strain

Earlier chapters have looked at the housing market, housing production and the building societies. This one draws these different aspects of owner-occupied housing provision together. It argues that many of the current problems of owner-occupation arise from the way in which it is provided. The difficulties, however, are structural – they cannot be resolved without substantial reform of owner-occupied housing provision.

Growing pressures on owner-occupiers

Households who are owner-occupiers are far from uniform in their social characteristics. As over 60 per cent of all households are owner-occupiers, this variety is not surprising. Average statistics showing that homeowners are better off than non-owners hide many pockets of strained economic circumstances within the tenure. With the expansion of owner-occupation, the absolute number of owner-occupiers living at the limit of their means has grown.

It is impossible to know precisely how many owners are in dire economic straits. The problem is submerged beneath most published statistics. When homeowners have high mortgage costs or face enormous repair bills, most get by. Living standards may be cut and repairs done inadequately but the actual incidence of hardship is never known.

One of the great advantages of individualized housing market systems for those opposed to state intervention, or state-inspired reforms, is precisely that many problems remain hidden and submerged. Occasionally, indications of the extent of economic difficulty do surface and disturb the picture of tranquillity. Mortgage defaults, a rising tide of disrepair and higher mortgage debt ratios, for instance, hint at growing economic distress.

Owner-occupation in Britain is organized in such a way that the economically strongest benefit from it most. They get the greatest tax relief, can afford repairs and to do-up cheap rundown houses, and they are in a position to move in order to optimize their housing circumstances. Households in the 25–55 age bracket, with members in good full-time employment and with small families, are best placed to gain the benefits of owner-occupation. But many people do not fall within that category, yet they have little choice but to become or remain owner-occupiers.

Expansion of owner-occupation from the 1920s onwards now means that a significant number of owner-occupiers are elderly and on low incomes. Many elderly owner-occupiers may have benefitted in the past from living in the tenure. Mortgages have been paid off, so their current housing outgoings are small, while rising housing prices may have enabled them to 'trade down' and realize a money gain which can be invested to bolster current income. Once having cashed in much of their money gain, elderly owners who move lose much of their potential financial flexibility. In the absence of a good continuing pension, such households depended on rentier income, and inflation is not kind to such income. Genteel poverty looms as an ever-present threat or reality for many such elderly home-owners.

Houses as well as people age, and require progressively more attention and money for their ailments. Not surprisingly, proportionately more elderly people live in older houses, and older houses are the ones that require most repair and improvement. Housing from the inter-war boom – about a quarter of the current owner-occupied stock – is now 50–60 years old and needs substantial, recurrent repair. Many owners of such housing, however, especially the elderly ones, cannot afford the rising costs of repair. Suburbia is slowly crumbling into the slums of tomorrow.

Successive house condition surveys show a rapid escalation of dilapidation in Britain's housing stock. Some of the greatest increases are in the owner-occupied stock. In 1981, only 62 per cent of owner-occupied houses required less than £1,000 worth of repairs; 17 per cent required between £1,000 and £2,500; and as much as 21 per cent needed more than £2,500-worth of repairs. Successive improvement schemes by governments have not succeeded in eradicating the repairs problem. At best they have only delayed the process of decay.

Marginal owners

Owner-occupation has never been just a wealthy person's housing tenure. But over the years, as housing opportunities in other tenures have declined, more and more households have had to purchase a house, even though it is virtually beyond their means. For ease of description, such householders can be called *marginal owners*. Mass unemployment and the restructuring of British industry have dashed other owner-occupiers' economic prospects, forcing them into the marginal category as well.

In the short-run, unemployment does not necessarily harm the owner-occupied housing market. Social security payments since the early 1960s have been available to cover the mortgage interest costs of the unemployed, although the Government now intends to water down this safeguard. Redundancy pay is also said to have been extensively used in house purchase or to pay off a mortgage. But over the longer-term, more and more owner-occupiers are facing a delicate balance between house purchase and mortgage default. During the early 1980s, although still a small proportion of total mortgages, mortgage arrears and possession doubled (from 1979–82).

The problems of marginal owner-occupiers are heightened by the higher mortgage debt ratios that were shown in the last chapter to exist in the 1980s. It is difficult to know whether the increase in debt is concentrated among economically strong or marginal owners. But any increase for marginal owners makes the task of repaying back a mortgage even more difficult.

Council house sales have added another marginal group to owner-occupation. Surveys show that most sitting tenant purchasers are aged 45 plus. Now they have substantial mortgages to pay off, even if the sales discounts have been exceedingly generous. Over the years, although the housing transferred from the council stock is generally better built than its private sector equivalent, their repair bills will also mount. Council tenant purchasers at some time will want to sell, and frequently they may find that their home has a poor market value.

Given this catalogue of marginal owners and increasing disrepair, it does not seem unreasonable to suggest that significant numbers of owner-occupiers could be in severe financial difficulty if the economy as a whole turns down. The essential problem is the age-old one of whether the private market can provide adequate housing at reasonable cost for the majority of the population. Until the remarkable success of owner-occupation in the late 1950s and 60s, few people thought it could. It now seems feasible that the success of owner-occupation may, in turn, be compartively short-lived – unless substantial changes are made to the way in which it is provided.

Housing production

Housing output for owner-occupation has singularly failed to expand to compensate for the cutbacks in council house building. Private housing completions have been averaging about 150,000 in recent years. There is no prospect of a substantial expansion in the near future, and even the current available forecasts could be optimistic, as they fail to consider the likelihood of sharp decline in the economy as a whole within the next few years. Overall housing output is running at less than two-thirds of forecast requirements. Each year of shortfall, in addition, adds to the cumulative deficit.

In the discussion of private housebuilding in Chapter 2, it was pointed out that speculative housebuilders face a crisis of production. Construction costs have been squeezed by the builders to their maximum, but only at the expense of the workforce (and to an extent, materials suppliers). That way of reducing costs cannot go on for ever, but the organization of the production process does not suggest that substantial productivity gains can be achieved to replace that cost-reducing effect. Meanwhile, the problems of construction quality remain. To cheapen their product, housebuilders are also likely to continue reducing space standards. To maintain profitability, they have to emphasize land development gains.

The seriousness of the dilemmas facing the volume housebuilders should not be underestimated. The restructuring of the industry into the hands of a few giant concerns is now virtually complete. The profitable opportunities open to innovative firms during that period of restructuring are now over as competitors have caught up. The outlook for profits does not look good. The next market downturn could easily bring about the spectacular failure of one or more of the volume builders, with repercussions for them all.

Given the increase in dilapidation, the repair and maintenance of owner-occupied housing is a growth industry. But housing repair and maintenance is the most inefficient sector of the building industry. Costs are high, skimped work rampant and the black economy rife. Repair and maintenance problems in the owner-occupied sector, therefore, do not relate solely to the state of the stock, but also to the cost and difficulty of getting anything done about it.

Building societies

As far as the housing market is concerned, the changing position of the building societies has meant that mortgage shortages are a thing of the past. But with more plentiful mortgages has come higher relative interest rates. Amongst other things, higher interest rates exacerbate the problems of marginal owners. Building societies might also start to encourage borrowers to take out unrealistically high loans.

Experience in the West German mortgage market after liberalization in the mid-1970s is worth noting. There, a rising housing market and strong selling campaigns by mortgage institutions led many owner-occupiers to take out high mortgage debts. Later, during the slump of the early 1980s, such debts brought considerable hardship and caused many mortgage defaults. The difficulties of such home-owners contributed substantially to a sharp fall in second-hand house prices in West Germany in the 1980s.

What happens in the next housing market downturn?

Predictions are dangerous things: they have a nasty habit of going wrong. The collapse of the owner-occupied housing market has been forecast before. It did, in fact, happen in 1974, but the then Labour Government helped pull owner-occupation back from the abyss by buying up a lot of the unsold stock of speculative builders. The present Government is unlikely to do the same. They are the champions of the private market, non-interference is their game-at least in theory, if not in practice. The British owner-occupied housing market seems to have a charmed life. In the recent recession of 1980–83, other Western European countries, such as West Germany and Italy, saw the collapse of their owner-occupied housing markets and of house prices in them. Output tumbled in Britain, but not house prices, and things quickly reverted to normal. But what will happen in the next downturn, or the one after that?

Too many factors can intervene to make accurate predictions possible. Yet the reasons why the British housing market avoided collapse in 1980–81 might not exist again in the future.

Most economic forecasts, not surprisingly, predict the onset of another recession in Britain sometime over the next few years. Some, like the London Business School, have even suggested that unemployment might rise to over five million; though the fall in oil prices at the end of 1985 made some of the forecasts more optimistic in the short-term. Such gloomy macro-economic prospects have substantial implications for the owner-occupied housing market. Housing demand, as was noted in Chapter 1, is strongly influenced by the rate of change of personal disposable incomes. In the next recession, the incomes of potential and existing owners might be severely squeezed – unlike in the early 1980s. If real incomes do fall, there will be a sudden contraction of demand in the housing market, which could spark off a price fall.

Once prices start to fall, demand could easily shrink even further. Existing owners will have less money gain with which to contemplate a new purchase, while new owners face the prospect of purchasing a depreciating asset. Most potential purchasers, therefore, are likely to hold off until prices stabilize. A cumulative housing market slump could emerge that takes years to break out of. The scenario just described did, in fact, occur in the Netherlands for five years from 1978 onwards – house prices fell by 40 per cent and for a long time transactions were at a low ebb.

Prospects for a sharp slump in the owner-occupied housing market have been intensified by the actions of the volume builders. For increased profitability, all are keen to expand their output. Optimistic views of future market trends become necessary to bolster expansion plans. Overhead costs are incurred that force firms onto the treadmill of expansion. Cutbacks in output then lead to rapid drops in profitability. Although today's large housebuilders are less likely to be forced into liquidation than their predecessors, they are not immune from collapse. If volume builders misjudge the timing and extent of the next slump and have rashly over-extended their borrowings, some spectacular failures may occur. If one of today's volume builders fails, thousands of houses will be thrown onto the market at one time. A flood of new houses sold under distressed circumstances would depress house prices even further than would have occurred anyway.

A structural crisis

Perhaps the scenario of a sharp fall in house prices is more than most owner-occupiers, housebuilders and building societies dare contemplate. If the owner-occupied market did collapse, it would certainly change the politics of owner-occupation. A dramatic fall in the housing market might never happen. What this chapter has tried to suggest is that the possibility of such a collapse is much greater than is generally felt.

Given the pronouncements of most housing experts and politicians, it would seem that nothing could ever go wrong with the owner-occupied housing market as a whole. Those views are simply untrue. A look across the Channel at some Western European countries is sufficient to dispel the idea that sharp falls in house prices and an almost total cessation of new housebuilding cannot occur. Housing markets do pick up again, but the processes of adjustment are extremely painful.

The basic problem within the British owner-occupied housing market is a structural one. All the agencies in the market have reacted to the characteristics of that market, particularly its instability, in their own interests, and in doing so have exacerbated the characteristics which they hoped to avoid.

One aspect of such structural adjustments is especially important. It concerns the level of housing output. Owner-occupied housing provision now is in such a state that any substantial increase in new housebuilding only takes place when prices rise rapidly. If prices do not rise at that rate, that output is not forthcoming. In the absence of any other form of housebuilding, shortages mount – eventually putting pressure on prices. Extremely high cost owner-occupation or very low housing output is the choice offered by the current structure of owner-occupied housing provision. The usual outcome is a muddy compromise somewhere between the two extremes.

Whatever the outcome, it spells hardship for many. The market is failing to deliver the goods and satisfy the housing needs of many.

Reform is an urgent necessity.

Chapter 5

Options for reform

The need for an overall perspective

Many reforms have been suggested for different parts of the owner-occupied system. Mortgage interest tax relief, conveyancing, improvement grants, land availability, mortgage finance and better transaction information are some of the topics that have been the subject of lively debate.

Two general features of the debates stand out clearly. First, the issues are seen in isolation. Feedback effects are rarely considered. Yet, as previous chapters have shown, it is difficult to understand the operations of one part of the owner-occupied system without seeing its place in the whole. Second, debates over particular reforms hardly ever recognize that the structure of owner-occupied housing provision is subject to continual change and, at present, is in severe crisis.

Some of the accepted wisdom about owner-occupation is likely to be shattered over the next few years. In its present form, owner-occupation cannot continue to satisfy the housing needs of the majority of the population, as it has been expected to do for the past 15 years or so. Transfers of the housing stock from other tenures have hidden the fact that for some time the present structure of owner-occupied housing provision has not been able to maintain a given level of housing standards for the population housed in the tenure, let alone improve those standards and take on an increasingly important role in housing the population as a whole. A backlog of years of low building rates, and insufficient repairs and improvement is gradually becoming apparent.

Owner-occupation has not been able to take over from public

sector housing programmes the roles of meeting the housing needs of the less well-off, of building sufficient housing for a geographically changing population and new household structures within it, and of improving or replacing the existing stock as it becomes worn-out or outmoded. Some successes have been achieved, but when viewed as the principal means of housing provision – which owner-occupation now is in Britain – owner-occupation cannot cope. The economic cost of its current structure of provision is too high. In one way or another all housing consumers end up paying the price. The worst hit are those who cannot afford the high prices induced by housing shortages. Yet everybody else, through higher housing costs, state subsidies or both, pays to maintain the current form of owner-occupation.

It could be argued that such conclusions are a vindication of outright opposition to owner-occupation. Rented housing, especially from public authorities, could be claimed to be 'superior'. Such a position, however, misunderstands both the basis of the critique of the current form of owner-occupation and, more importantly, that characteristics of housing tenures vary depending on the social institutions associated with them. Owner-occupation can be changed as much as other tenures by altering the way in which it is provided – the institutions, tax regimes, costs and obligations associated with the tenure. The simple opposition of tenures ignores such possibilities.

There is nothing inherently superior in either owning or renting, despite frequent protestations to the contrary. Because households' circumstances, experience and means vary and change over time, a guiding principle of any major housing reform in Britain should be to encourage variety and choice in the way in which people consume housing and in the associated costs. What is important is to remove the negative aspects of current tenure forms – their inefficiencies, high costs and lack of correspondence to peoples' housing needs.

What follows is a set of proposals for radical reform of the current structure of owner-occupied housing provision. It is based on the principle of maintaining the basic property rights of owner-occupiers in the context of removing the tenure from the unregulated market and the control of the agencies currently operating there. The proposals imply major structural change and an extension of public ownership. The proposals are meant as suggestions for change, rather than a hard-and-fast political programme. They illustrate the potential for transforming housing provision in this country. Detailed political circumstances would have to determine the precise details of any major reform. Substantial changes, however, are required if housing provision in Britain is to break out of the debilitating straightjacket in which it is now encased. A later section will argue why more limited piecemeal reforms have little chance of success.

A programme for change

The basic proposals can be presented as an integrated 10-point programme. Many of the points are self-explanatory. An explanation of the basis of the programme follows.

1 Housebuilding by publicly accountable bodies, organized on a regional and local basis. These bodies could be state-run, at national or local level, quasi-independent or supervised co-operatives.

2 These new building enterprises would not operate like the traditional public corporation model of nationalized industries. Instead, they would operate on broader social criteria of meeting local housing needs, fulfilling pre-given quality standards, improving the productive capability of the industry, and productive efficiency (measured through a combination of physical and financial criteria).

3 Recognition that building workers are the principal productive resource in housebuilding: new forms of employment based on decasualization of building work, improved pay and working conditions, an emphasis on quality as much as speed of work, extensive training and retraining programmes.

4 Public ownership of land, with a new form of leasehold under which buildings could be owned by their existing owners or others, but with stipulated obligations associated with the transfer of ownership. No general compensation to previous landowners, but special hardship funds for land-users adversely affected by the ownership change.

5 Planned local programmes of new housebuilding, repair

and improvement, and redevelopment. These programmes to be based on assessments of local housing needs and available resources in terms of local and national criteria. Account to be taken of all housing tenures. User participation in determining the programmes should be obligatory. Housebuilding to be linked to the proposals of the plans.

6 New housing credit institutions dispensing funds to owner-occupiers and other housing institutions. These should be locally or regionally based, non-profit-making bodies restricted to operating in housing and related fields. Restrictions to be imposed on their size to avoid the problems of institutional aggrandizement.

7 The new housing institutions to evolve operating procedures which recognize the need for public accountability and democratic control. Local scale and social audit criteria are an important basis for such procedures.

8 Reform of the exchange process. Removal of conveyancing by use of 'log book' leaseholds issued and updated for each property by the relevant land authority. House sales and moves in other tenures in a locality to be co-ordinated through a 'housing exchange', using computerized information systems and an extensive network of local offices or housing 'shops'. Each offer of housing for sale or rent to be backed up by an independently validated structural survey, and an assessment of the costs of repairing defects or a commitment to undertake the works, when necessary.

9 Regulated house prices: prices on the housing market over the long term would be influenced by the prices at which new houses were sold. There would still be a need to have a pricing strategy towards short-term imbalances between supply and demand. The level of prices would depend on contemporary circumstances but some guiding criteria would be specified. The pricing criteria for new houses, perhaps, for reasons of political expediency should not be pitched so that existing owners face recurrent losses in the value of their dwellings. The profits made from new house sales could be used to fund new experiments in building

techniques, administrative procedures, etc, or to subsidize housing programmes in other tenures.

Second-hand sales could either be unregulated or – preferably – regulated, with prices set to take account of new house prices, social criteria and local supply and demand balances. Administered prices would limit the possibility of sharp bursts of house price inflation, although black market payments would be an ever present danger. The 'log book' system should limit the possibility of recurrent black market transactions.

10 Taxation reforms should be tailored to the new organization of provision. Mortgage tax relief could stay, but, to limit the incentive for existing owners to move and to direct subsidies where they are most needed, tax relief should be restricted to the mortgage of the household's first house purchase only. Considerable savings would thereby ensue for the Exchequer.

Another tax reform could be a revamped stamp duty, repackaged in the style of a sales tax. The sales tax would vary depending on the rate of house price increase, both discouraging price rises and syphoning off part of the inflationary gains made.

The importance of relating owner-occupation to housing needs

To have any influence over the housing made available for owner-occupation and over the quality and costs of that housing, it is necessary to control the housing market. The proposals above are designed to do that, and to develop institutional forms that maximize the accountability of housing institutions to people's housing needs and to improving the productive capability of the housebuilding industry.

Owner-occupation as a tenure is not in question. Instead, reforms are suggested to ways under which owner-occupied houses are produced and traded. The tenure would no longer be a way of making money for a lucky few at the expense of others, but a means by which people's housing needs could be satisfied, without the loss of either freedom of choice or personal ownership rights. To do this, the institutions associated with owner-occupied housing provision need to be altered, and virtually all of them are in urgent need of reform – including private land ownership, housebuilding, mortgage finance, and the exchange professionals (like estate agents).

The object is to make owner-occupation cheaper and transactions more efficient, and for it to be feasible to alter the range and types of housing available in the tenure so that those with greatest housing need can be catered for. As the enormous financial gains made in the housing development process would no longer be channelled to a handful of landowners and to the shareholders of speculative builders, they could be used to reduce the cost and improve the condition of people's housing.

The importance of controlling housing production

New forms of housebuilding are key elements of the suggested proposals. They are necessary in order to make it possible to take housebuilding out of the constraints of profit-making. New housebuilding, although only a relatively small proportion of total owner-occupied market transactions, was argued earlier to be the key determinant of prices and the types of housing available in the market because it is the source of new supply. Control of housing production, therefore, is essential for any influence over owner-occupation as a whole and the conditions under which houses are bought and sold. Through control of housebuilding, effective decisions could be made on output levels, the types of housing built and long-term trends in house prices.

Nationalization of speculative housebuilders is not being suggested. As speculative housebuilders own very few productive assets, nationalization would not achieve much – particularly as their land banks would anyway be subject to the land nationalization proposals.

It was argued earlier that housebuilding for owner-occupation has its current characteristics because speculative housebuilders' drive for profits pushes their actions towards marketing, land dealing and development at the expense of the requirements of production. Productive activities have to be flexible to satisfy marketing and land development needs, with disastrous long-term consequences for housing production as a whole. It is essential, therefore, that the new types of housebuilder do not operate on profit-maximizing criteria; otherwise the same problems will be reproduced in new institutional guises. Instead, the central objectives of the building agencies should be to meet housing needs and to further the productive capabilities of the housebuilding industry. Certain consequences stem from these principles which lead on to other points in the proposed programme.

Looking at the issue of meeting housing needs first, clearly some form of economic and social planning is required. This is necessary to assess housing needs and to link housing requirements into wider economic and social priorities and constraints. Some effective planning at the national level is required in this context. It is widely recognized that governments' panic short-term cutting back of housing programmes, which occur in the absence of effective plans, have been highly disruptive. But it is equally important that plans are not dictated from above. Housing users should have an effective voice in the development of housing strategies and in detailed issues like design. Effective participation can only be achieved at the local level rather than nationally. It should also be a central plank of such activities that people in distinct localities can choose, through the process of political representation and within nationally laid down minima, different levels of output, mixes of tenure, house types and standards.

Precisely what spatial area is meant by the term 'local' depends on the issue in question. Detailed design issues can be dealt with at a very localized level (although hopefully the quality of the new housing produced and the new building agencies' sensitivity to user needs will avoid the need for potential consumers to attend endless design meetings). Other issues related to planned housebuilding programmes would have to operate at a wider level, say, the municipality or sub-region.

With regard to the new housebuilding enterprises, the issue of accountability again suggests a local or regional perspective rather than a single national housebuilder. Similarly, different types of organization could be tried to see which worked best, or which related to specific areas of work or housebuilding needs. Repair and maintenance, for instance, is better organized on different lines from new building. So it is likely that more than one housebuilding organization would operate in an area, some state-owned and some not. The need to have sufficient work in hand to maintain continuity of work puts a limit on the degree to which decentralization can proceed. A balance would need to be struck between the advantages of local accountability and the benefits of economies of scale.

To meet the dual objectives of accountability and improving the productive capability of the housebuilding industry, the new building agencies should operate on the basis of what is often called a 'social audit'. A 'social audit' implies a mixed set of financial and physical criteria as operating targets for the enterprises, rather than an attempt to reduce economic performance to one unitary measure. The numbers of houses built, their quality and type, consumer satisfaction, the contribution to local housing plans, amongst other things, could be used to measure the output of the enterprise, as well as the more usual one of net revenue obtained. In terms of productive capability, again, a series of physical measures might cast more light and direct the enterprise's efforts in the most socially beneficial ways, rather than sole emphasis on cost. Examples of physical measures include levels of investment in new plant and equipment, training programmes for building workers, innovations in methods and designs, and safety record.

Efficiency measures could also take a physical form – labour hours required to build a dwelling and utilization rates for equipment are just two such examples. Apart from being publicly available for examination, the social audits could be scrutinized and compared by an official set of assessors with powers to instruct the building enterprises to improve their performance.

The great advantage of such building enterprises is that within them production can be continuous and building workers can be treated as the central productive asset that they are. The enterprises have a disincentive to use construction inputs on a casual basis, as that would mitigate against their need to achieve all the criteria of a social audit. With continuous production, opportunities for substantial improvements in productive efficiency and innovations in building methods arise.

Similarly, building workers can be adequately trained and paid, and encouraged to put emphasis on quality as much as speed. Much of the current problems of housing production stem from the way in which speculative housebuilders treat building workers. Improvements in their working conditions and remuneration are not simply much needed for the workers themselves, but actually lead to a more productive industry. In this respect, it is worth noting that some of Europe's most efficient construction industries are in countries where building workers have strong and effective union representation, Sweden being the best known, if not the only, example.

Where would the revenue come from to finance these institutions? Partially, it would come from house sales and income from other housing projects (there is no reason why they should build for owner-occupation alone). But, in a situation where house and land prices were administratively regulated and where profit maximizing was not the only operating criteria, they could easily need other sources of revenue. This could either come from a redistribution of surpluses between housebuilding institutions, from the surpluses of land agencies, or from the government via the receipts of the house sales tax or other funds. Given the substantial revenues derived as profits and land prices in the current structure of owner-occupied housing provision, the switching of those flows of funds to housebuilding itself should not impose extra costs on the economy, and much should be left for other uses, including housing projects.

Reforming the other institutions

Apart from housebuilding, the other reforms are designed to redistribute the financial benefits of owner-occupation, to lower its cost and to prevent economic sabotage of the new housebuilding enterprises. The public ownership of land is addressed to all three elements. Reform of housing exchange considerably reduces the cost of house purchase and sale, gives consumers far more information than is currently available, and aids the process of stabilizing the housing market away from the neverending cycle of boom and slump. The break-up of the big building societies and a refocus on mortgage lending to meet housing needs, instead of as a basis for never-ending expansion, would lower interest rates, make mortgages more readily available to groups currently subject to building society discrimination, and remove the large potential for sabotage of housing reforms that the building societies currently wield.

The problems of limited reforms of owner-occupation

It is widely accepted that the current structure of owner-occupied housing provision needs reform in one way or another. Most proposals deal with only one aspect of the process of provision, while neglecting others. This section provides a brief review of the difficulties faced by the some of most well-known ones.

● Abolition of mortgage interest tax relief

If any currently debated housing policy reform has been damned with the claim that it is politically impracticable, it is the abolition of mortgage tax relief; yet it is the most commonly accepted reform of owner-occupation, and it said to be urgently needed both on grounds of social justice and to reduce the burden on public expenditure. The never-ending escalation of this subsidy makes the likelihood of reform greater each year. Changing reality has a remarkable facility for turning the politically impossible into the possible.

Abolition of mortgage tax relief is seen as a panacea which removes all the injustices and inefficiencies currently associated with owner-occupation. Such sweeping claims are false. Abolition of the subsidy does little for the structural problems of owner-occupation discussed earlier. If anything, it exacerbates them. House prices would fall as a result of its withdrawal. Yet the market would still be as unstable, and housebuilders would still face the same crisis of production – except that house purchasers would be even less able to afford to buy their products. Withdrawal of mortgage interest tax relief, by itself, might initially improve the distribution of subsidies, but it would also lead to a growing housing shortage.

In addition, the timing of the abolition of mortgage interest tax relief when undertaken in the absence of more far-reaching reforms faces almost insuperable problems. Sudden withdrawal would lead to much personal hardship amongst owner-occupiers, with possibly the total collapse of the housebuilding industry and severe strain on the building societies as well. The solution to this difficulty is usually couched in terms of a gradual whittling away of the subsidy. Gradualism, however, has its own problems. Politically, the impact of a particular measure is lost: gradualism can easily be reversed by an opportunistic vote-catching government in the future.

Neo-classical economists have come out with a variation on mortgage interest tax relief abolition. They suggest that owner-occupiers derive an imputed income from the rent they, as housing users, implicitly pay themselves as housing owners. Like all income, such implicit rental payments should be taxed, they suggest. Mortgage interest tax relief could stay, but each year owner-occupiers would pay a percentage of the current value of their house in tax.

As a fiscal reform, the proposal faces most of the difficulties of abolishing mortgage interest tax relief, plus a few extra ones of its own. As imputed income does not actually exist, there is no actual current income out of which to pay the annual tax. The tax is, in practice, a wealth tax to be paid out of current income. For some owner-occupiers the continuance of mortgage tax relief would offset the tax but, for most, the tax would lead to a sharp reduction in current disposable income. The impact of the tax would be disproportionately felt by marginal owners – either recent purchasers, or those who have fallen on hard times, or the elderly on fixed low incomes. As such it is a recipe for social injustice, mortgage defaults, forced sales and disrepair. The resulting subsidies and exemptions, likely to be introduced to overcome some of the problems, would soon become incredibly complex and negate the initial neatness of the proposal.

● Reforms associated with marginal owners
   and dilapidated houses

A variety of schemes have been suggested, and some implemented, which shift the distribution of subsidies towards those who most need them. First-time buyers have been given special subsidies and improvement grants have been directed at the worst parts of the stock. Again, in isolation such schemes have only limited effect, despite their enormous cost.

Tipping the subsidy scales in favour of marginal owners increases the demand for owner-occupation, without altering the way in which it is supplied. So such subsidies help to push up house prices. As the subsidies are focused on particular sectors of the market, the prices of houses for marginal buyers rise the most. Marginal owners consequently are not the prime beneficiaries of subsidies directed at them.

Subsidies towards repair and improvement are directed at particular parts of the private housing stock. The effect of subsidies on the standard of the existing stock is difficult to judge as there are two possible secondary effects of their existence. The first is that subsidies may push up the prices of houses for which they can be obtained. If an area is gentrifying, for instance, the declaration of a general improvement area will primarily bring a windfall, through rising house prices, to existing owners and developers who do-up property. The subsidies are unlikely to induce much additional improvement as it would have occurred anyway. Secondly, like garages which repair accident-damaged cars and demand high prices in the knowledge that an insurance company is paying, builders may demand high charges because of the existence of grants. The extent to which they do depends on the degree of competition, but experience has shown it can occur quite frequently.

Improvement subsidies, as they currently exist, face the same difficulties as other owner-occupation subsidies. They are directed only towards stimulating the demand for improvement. They have little or no effect on the way in which improvement is done. The small-time, inefficient builders who generally undertake such work simply get a boost in the demand for their services. This may push up their profits and it may lead to more improvement work, but it fails to tackle the fundamental problems of production in that sphere.

● Exchange reforms

One area where the need for reform has been stressed in recent years is the process of buying and selling dwellings. The solicitors' monopoly of conveyancing is under attack and is likely to be weakened, but not eradicated, in the near future. Demands have been made for the Land Registry to be open to the public. The present haphazard way purchasers find out about the physical state of properties has been criticized. Proposals have been put forward by which sellers would have to provide a 'warranty' style package containing details of their rights to title and a structural survey of the dwelling. Estate agents' inefficient and expensive services have also been subject to much critical comment, and reforms have been proposed ranging from local authority takeover to national computer-based information systems.

In terms of reforming the current institutional structure of owner-occupation, the exchange professionals – especially solicitors, estate agents and surveyors – seem in the weakest position to defend their entrenched interests. Reform of at least some aspects of the archaic exchange process is likely over the next few years, and it is to be welcomed.

As with the rest of the structure of owner-occupied housing provision, reform of the exchange process may have some unforeseen consequences. The problems do not negate the need for reform but indicate the significance of interlinkages in the housing market. If the outrageous transaction costs of buying and selling houses are reduced, and the exchange process simplified and speeded up, two consequences for the level of market activity may emerge. First, some of the money saved by purchasers may be used to fund house purchase itself. Such a stimulation to demand may push up house prices, negating some of the effect of the savings in transaction costs. Second, the speeding up of the exchange process will remove one of the constraints on the escalation of prices and transactions during booms. At present, at high levels of market activity, the exchange process tends to clog up – slowing down the turnover of houses. Removal of such impediments may enable booms to go to greater heights or to occur more frequently. After the booms will come even sharper downturns. The instability of the market, in other words, could become even more pronounced than at present, unless measures are taken to control it. That requires substantial structural reform.

● Bolstering speculative builders

Housebuilders have done well in recent years in getting more land released through the planning system. They would like more and much cheaper land. But it is difficult to see how more land release and lower land prices would help them transform the way in which houses are built. Housebuilders' profits would be given a boost by the windfall of extra cheap land, and their land banks topped up. Construction costs and the organization of production remain unaffected.

Subsidies to speculative housebuilders could be tried, although as chapter 2 pointed out, they already receive many implicit ones. Problems arise here as it is difficult to envisage a subsidy system that alters the way houses are produced rather than merely subsidizing existing construction costs.

How feasible is the proposed restructuring of owner-occupation?

The package of reforms of owner-occupied housing provision suggested here is based on an analysis of the current operation of home ownership in Britain, and the problems it faces. The aim is to develop the benefits people derive from living in the tenure, whilst removing the blatant inefficiencies and injustices that currently exist. Unlike other proposals for reform, emphasis has not been put on the impact of government subsidy and taxation policies, instead blame has been firmly directed towards the institutions that currently dominate owner-occupied housing provision and the consequences, often unintended, of their mutual interaction.

Widespread institutional change, nevertheless, seems politically difficult to envisage. In addition, the proposals here suggest a much greater public sector involvement in housing provision and the building industry. Powerful entrenched interests are threatened, and they are formidable lobbyists. Concerted attempts have also been made in recent years to discredit the idea of direct state intervention in the provision of goods and services: they seem to have convinced the leaderships of all the major political parties, if no-one else. Why try and campaign for major changes in owner-occupation in such bleak circumstances?

A number of points can be made in reply to such pessimism. In the first place, far from being realistic, a position which argues for the impossibility of major change is patently unrealistic. As this book has pointed out, major change is already taking place in the way in which owner-occupation is provided, and governments whether they like it or not are being forced to respond. The argument, in reality, is not whether there should be major structural change in owner-occupied housing provision, but rather in whose interests should those changes be implemented. At the moment, most housing users are bearing the cost of change through their housing circumstances or tax payments and seeing few of the benefits.

The past five years, furthermore, have seen a major legislative programme towards owner-occupation, which has taken in council house sales, planning and land availability, raising the limit on mortgage interest tax relief, inner city housing programmes, conveyancing and the building societies. There has been no rolling back of state intervention or expenditure in the housing sphere, just a redirection of emphasis away from the needs of users towards those of the institutions associated with owner-occupation. In part, the redirection was for ideological reasons, but a major factor was a profound ignorance of how owner-occupied housing provision currently works.

The need for further state intervention to cope with the enormity of the current housing crisis in Britain is widely recognized. All the major political parties to varying degrees intend simply to spend large sums of money, as though the current forms of housing provision are like old cars that can be patched up and temporarily put on the road again. Reforming the institutions of housing provision is likely to provide far better results, and be a lot cheaper.

One scenario raised earlier was of a collapse in the owner-occupied housing market, with falling prices, bankrupt homeowners, and failing housebuilders and financial institutions. Current developments are increasing the possibility of such a collapse, and substantial reform will be forced on governments if it happened. The panic measures introduced then, however, are unlikely to be satisfactory. A wiser move would be to introduce change now.

Another objection to the reforms proposed here could be that they are hopelessly expensive. Yet, as long as a sensible approach is taken towards land nationalization, the initial costs need not be very great and over the longer-term costs would be far less than now for both the consumer and the Exchequer. Land apart, no large scale programme of nationalization with its attendant compensation costs is proposed, instead organizations would be built up from scratch. There would obviously be set-up costs, but they would be little different from those associated with any large scale building programme.

The main economic implication of the reform would be to redirect the financial flows in owner-occupation away from the processes associated with house buying and selling, land dealing, property and land ownership, and mortgage finance, towards the effective use of scarce productive resources to provide decent housing for all.

Whether anything is politically feasible also depends on the extent of campaigning for it. The issues of housing shortages and the injustices of the current arrangements have been kept on the political agenda because of campaigns in various forms. Unfortunately, in my opinion, too much campaigning emphasis is put on tenure. The right to buy or the right to rent have been championed, with less consideration given to what you end up getting and who pays the bill. Within tenures, subsidies and taxation are all that seem to matter, whereas in reality I would suggest that it is delivery systems that count.

A radical restructuring of owner-occupation on the lines proposed might seem a tall order even when political circumstances are favourable, which now they are clearly not. But the extent of the current structural crisis, and the almost zero effect of more limited reforms, make it essential.

References

To improve readability the normal academic practice of citing reference sources was not used in this text. The purpose of these references is to provide a brief guide to the literature.

The arguments in this book are mainly a summary and introduction to those made in my book *Housing policy and economic power: the political economy of owner-occupation*, published by Methuen in 1983. See also my 'Coming to terms with owner-occupation', *Capital and class* 24, 1985, and *Mortgage finance in Britain and West Germany*, M. Ball, M. Martens and M. Harloe, *Progress and planning*, 1986.

International comparisons of forms of housing provision are few and far between. (There are more of housing policy, which in isolation is not very illuminating.)

M. Martens 'Owner occupation in Western Europe: problems and prospects', *Environment and planning A*, 1985, is a good introduction to the nature of owner-occupation in other European countries. P. Dickens, S. Duncan, M. Goodwin and F. Gray *Housing, states and localities*, Methuen, 1985, gives a somewhat idealized view of the Swedish system of homeownership.

J. Kemeny presents a critique of the international emphasis in housing policy on owner-occupation in *The myth of home-ownership*, Routledge and Kegan Paul, 1980.

Homeownership in Britain, with a strong emphasis on state policies towards it, is covered extensively in one of the many housing textbooks that have blossomed over the past few years. A good, if tediously dry, introduction to the consumption and finance aspects of homeownership still remains the technical appendices of the Housing Policy Green Paper of 1977, published by HMSO.

Proposals for the reform of the tax and subsidy arrangements as a panacea for the problems of owner-occupation abound; M. King and A. Atkinson 'Housing policy, taxation and reform', *Midland Bank Review*, Spring, 1980, and J. Ermisch *Housing finance: who gains?*, Policy Studies Institute, 1984, are good starting points. Studies of the determinants of house prices have been surveyed and summarized in *The determination of house prices*, published by the Building Societies Association in 1984. J. Doling, V. Karn and B. Stafford, *Behind with the mortgage*, National Consumer Council, 1985, examine the growing incidence of mortgage defaults and arrears. T. Gough's *The economics of building societies*, Macmillan, 1982, casts a critical view over the operations of the building societies. Shelter's own magazine *Roof* publishes short articles that help in keeping up with the current issues associated with owner-occupation.

Concerning data, the government's quarterly and annual *Housing and construction statistics* are the prime source, though the present government has reduced the available information and charges a hefty price for what remains. The Building Societies Association quarterly bulletin is another good source of data on owner-occupation. Articles in the bulletin frequently provide additional information, and the ingenuity displayed defending the societies against all criticism, real and imagined, can often be amusing, even though it has a more serious intent. The Nationwide's *Housing trends* is another useful source of data on house prices and the characteristics of homeowners who borrow from them.

◆ SPECIAL ◆ OFFER!!

Filling the Empties

SHORT LIFE HOUSING & HOW TO DO IT

By Ross Fraser
of the Empty Property Unit

This exciting new book is the first comprehensive how-to-do-it guide to short life housing — the temporary use of empty property for homeless people. It covers:

★ **Setting up a short life co-operative** ★ **Negotiating for houses** ★ **Short life lettings and the law** ★ **Obtaining funding** ★ **How to meet statutory housing standards** ★ **Allocation and equal opportunities** ★ **Moving on to permanent housing** ★ **The dangers of asbestos** ★

This book is technical without ever being dull, well illustrated and is an essential resource for **local authorities** looking for alternatives to bed and breakfast hotels; **housing associations** seeking to extend their activity with temporary housing schemes; **short life housing groups** seeking to improve their service and **homeless people** hoping to set up housing co-operatives to meet their housing needs.

Copies are available from SHELTER, 157 Waterloo Road at the discount price of £4.95 (post free — money with orders please).

An EXTRA DISCOUNT to £3.95 per copy is available on orders of five or more copies.